ANIMALS OF THE GREAT BARRIER REEF

by Martha E. H. Rustad

raintree
a Capstone company — publishers for children

Raintree is an imprint of Capstone Global Library Limited, a company incorporated in England and Wales having its registered office at 264 Banbury Road, Oxford, OX2 7DY – Registered company number: 6695582

www.raintree.co.uk
myorders@raintree.co.uk

Edited by Jaclyn Jaycox
Designed by Hilary Wacholz
Original illustrations © Capstone Global Library Limited 2022
Picture research by Jo Miller
Production by Spencer Rosio
Originated by Capstone Global Library Ltd
Printed and bound in India

978 1 3982 2488 9 (hardback)
978 1 3982 2487 2 (paperback)

British Library Cataloguing in Publication Data
A full catalogue record for this book is available from the British Library.

Acknowledgements
We would like to thank the following for permission to reproduce photographs: Alamy: redbrick.com, 11, Suzanne Long, 19; Capstone: Eric Gohl, 5; Dreamstime: Brian Scantlebury, 15, Geotrac, 21, James Robins, 13; Shutterstock: Coral Brunner, 16, HotFlash, 7, Jemma Craig, 10, Jukka Jantunen, 14, Martin Maun, 4, Mike Workman, 6, Nico Faramaz, 12, Ogurtsov, Cover, Pete Niesen, 17, Tracey Jones Photography, 9, 18, Vlasov_38RUS, 1.
Design elements: Capstone; Shutterstock: Vlasov_38RUS.

Every effort has been made to contact copyright holders of material reproduced in this book. Any omissions will be rectified in subsequent printings if notice is given to the publisher.

Contents

Words in **bold** are in the glossary.

THE GREAT BARRIER REEF

Blue waves wash over the Great Barrier Reef. It is found in the Pacific Ocean. It sits off the coast of Australia. The reef stretches for about 2,300 kilometres (1,400 miles).

The Great Barrier Reef is a group of coral reefs. It is made by tiny animals called **coral polyps**. Many plants and animals live there.

North America

Europe

Asia

Africa

South America

Australia

Antarctica

N

W   E

S

Great Barrier Reef

REEF ANIMALS

Coral polyps live in groups. Their bodies are soft. They have hard skeletons. One end sticks to a reef or rock. Its mouth is at the other end. Around its mouth are arms called **tentacles**. They grab floating food.

tentacle

More than 450 kinds of coral live in the Great Barrier Reef. These animals leave behind their skeletons when they die. The reefs grow slowly over millions of years.

Clown fish live in **anemones**. Anemones look like plants. But they are animals. Anemones sting other fish. Slime covers a clown fish's skin. The slime keeps it safe from the anemone's sting.

Anemones stick to a coral reef. They eat fish and other animals. Clown fish and anemones share food. Anemones protect clown fish. Clown fish keep anemones clean. They work together to survive.

Sea turtles swim near the Great Barrier Reef. They eat jellyfish and crabs. They eat sea grasses too.

Female sea turtles make nests on tiny islands between reefs. They dig holes in the sand. They lay eggs and cover them. Baby sea turtles hatch. They crawl to the water. Young sea turtles grow up in the ocean.

Manta rays glide through the ocean water. They have wide, flat bodies. Their fins can reach as wide as 7 metres (23 feet).

gills

fin

Manta rays eat tiny plants and animals. They eat fish too. Fins near a ray's mouth sweep in water and food. Then the water goes out through its **gills**.

Sea birds called terns swoop over the Great Barrier Reef. They catch fish and crabs swimming below.

Terns raise their young on islands. They make nests out of bits of coral, plants and seaweed. Their eggs blend in with the nests. This keeps the eggs safe. Terns spit up fish to feed their babies with.

LIFE ON THE REEF

The Great Barrier Reef is a good home for animals. Colourful corals give little fish places to hide. Big fish swim close to catch little fish. They leave behind tiny fish bits. Corals eat the tiny bits. Each animal is important to each other.

Earth's **climate** is changing. Our planet is getting warmer. The oceans are heating up. Heat can harm coral polyps. It can turn the colourful coral white. This is called bleaching.

bleached coral

People are working hard to help stop coral bleaching. They do studies to find ways to stop climate change. We can work to protect the Great Barrier Reef. We can help save the animals that call it home.

Fight climate change

The planet is slowly getting warmer. Oceans are getting warmer too. We can all help to save the Great Barrier Reef.

What you can do

1. Think about the ways you and your family get around. Cars use a lot of fuel. They put gases into the air. These gases can trap heat and make the planet warmer. Try walking, riding a bike or getting a bus instead.

2. Try to use less electricity. Turn off lights when you leave a room. Unplug things when you aren't using them.

3. Use less water. Turn off the tap while brushing your teeth. Have short showers or shallow baths.

Glossary

anemone animal with a soft body and tentacles; anemones stay attached to a reef or rock

climate usual weather that occurs in a place

coral polyp ocean animal that helps make coral reefs

gill slit on the side of a fish used for breathing

tentacle long, flexible limb (like a leg or an arm) used for moving, feeling and grabbing

Find out more

Books

All About Oceans (Habitats), Christina Mia Gardeski (Raintree, 2018)

Marine Habitats Around the World (Exploring Earth's Habitats), Phillip Simpson (Raintree, 2020)

Read All About the Oceans (Read All About It), Jaclyn Jaycox (Raintree, 2021)

Websites

greatbarrierreef.com.au/great-barrier-reef-facts-for-kids/
Visit the official Great Barrier Reef website.

www.dkfindout.com/uk/animals-and-nature/jellyfish-corals-and-anemones/corals/
Learn more about corals with DKfindout!

Index